Released tells a story o[f] [vi]ctor[ious]
rescue. The author op[enly] [s]ha[res how she was]
released from a stronghold responsible for a very
dark season in her life. Her transparency engages and
challenges us to enter the battle for freedom promised
through Christ. Anyone who has experienced the
darkness of depression in their soul, or debilitating
fear in the form of anxiety, should walk with Tina on
her journey. This story recounts the reality of spiritual
warfare fought and won with divinely powerful
weapons. "For though we walk in the flesh, we are not
waging war according to the flesh. For the weapons of
our warfare are not of the flesh but have divine power
to destroy strongholds" II Corinthians 10: 3–4.

—Chuck Hannaford, Ph.D.
Executive Director, HeartLife Professional Soul-Care

Clinical Professor of Biblical Counseling
The Southern Baptist Theological Seminary

Author, *Picking up the Pieces Handbook:
Creating a Dynamic Soul-Care Ministry in Your Church*

Released

Released

SETTING YOUR SPIRIT FREE

FROM DEPRESSION AND ANXIETY

TINA THOMPSON

EXPANDED EDITION

eternity
resources

Eternity Resources books may be ordered through
booksellers or by contacting:

ℯ ⱡ ℯ r n i t y
resources

A division of Eternity Communications, Inc.
467 W 2nd Street
Lexington, KY 40507
eternityresources.com
(859) 327-3337

ISBN: 978-0-692-93108-0

Acknowledgments

A special note of thanks first to my Lord and Savior: I would have not made it through without Him—my strength and the One I run to.

Then to my wonderful husband, Larry, who lived through this time in my life and was willing to pray with me, and for me, and always let me know He would be there for me, and we would get through this together with God's help. And the part I love most— for his willingness to stand up and be the spiritual leader and always point our family to look to God.

And last but not least, our two wonderful daughters, Ginger and Bridget, who have made this life worth living and who are not afraid to challenge me, "Is this the way God would handle or look at things?" Thank you, girls, for being such wonderful and godly young women.

Contents

Preface

I know that God can free you from depression and anxiety. How can I be so sure?

Let me tell you the story of a girl named Ty. One of seven children, she was born into a family with little means. As a matter fact, she had special lunch tickets at school, but she didn't even realize that it was because they were poor. Her mother was very clever telling her that her lunch ticket was special and had a different color.

Ty watched her father physically and verbally abuse their mother and all the children to the point that she would go to bed in the evenings covering her ears so as not to hear the physical and mental abuse.

From ages 7 to 9, Ty was sexually molested by a family member. This abuse became something that would change her life for many years. She would become a people pleaser so that she would be loved for something other than her body. She became nonconfrontational and would avoid conflict at any cost.

By age 9, she began having panic and anxiety attacks to the point that she would lay in bed at night and just pray and pray and pray and panic and panic and panic, knowing she couldn't tell her father or he would get angry and probably hit her or maybe tell her to suck it up and go to bed.

She remembers at age 16 panicking so badly that she got up the nerve to go to her parents' room one night. She went to her mother's side of the bed and told her she was scared. It was storming at the time, so for some reason it was OK to be afraid of a storm, but not to have panic attacks, so she just let her parents believe it was the storm that made her afraid, and they allowed her to stay on the first level of the house with them.

At age 17, she left home as soon as she graduated to get out of the abusive life in which she was living.

She moved to a different state, and the thought of a different life and things she had never seen or known before intrigued her. It also made her afraid. But the hope of a peaceful life was more powerful than the fear of leaving.

At age 18, she was looking for someone to love her unconditionally and because she was looking for that love, she became willing to give up her body thinking someone would surely love her if she willingly gave herself to them. So she became an unwed pregnant girl, very scared and feeling alone, not knowing what to do.

At age 19, she became a mother for the first time and married the boy who had gotten her pregnant. Knowing this boy for only a year, she wasn't sure what she was getting herself into.

At age 21, she began a deep, bottomless depression, feeling unworthy and unloved, believing that her husband must have married her not for love but because of the baby. That led to further feelings of depression and anxiety.

It led to wanting to kill her child. One time, she even went into her child's bedroom with a knife in her hand, thinking of killing the child. Ty did this while the child was peacefully sleeping because part of her didn't want to scare the child. Yet, her mind was conflicted with the horrible thoughts of harming her child. Because Ty's mind was torn, she began thinking there was no need for Ty to stay alive. She was no good to anyone. Ty began thinking of ways to end her life. To this day, she is surprised she didn't carry it out.

At age 22, she became pregnant for the second time and had a miscarriage. She had feelings of guilt because she really had not wanted this child. She was afraid that the depression and fear would go deeper, and she could barely function and perform normal, day-to-day life as it was. She could not shower. She could not do dishes. She could barely eat, and she just did not want the pressure of anything else on her.

At age 23, she became pregnant again, still fearful the depression would get worse but also worried she would have another miscarriage. She found out she was carrying twins at six and a half months into the pregnancy. She had complications and learned that one of the twins had died. She carried this twin full-term in order for the other twin to survive. That played a lot of tricks on her brain and deepened her depression knowing that she was caring a dead fetus in her body. It was very traumatic to a fragile mind.

"What is wrong with me," she would wonder. "I can't do this life anymore," she would tell herself.

After the birth of her second child, she was told she had a blood condition and that her body would abort any future children.

Ty was diagnosed manic depressive/bipolar disorder by a doctor when she was 29. She felt like

God had sent her to this particular doctor because his wife had suffered with the same diagnosis, and he had experience with what to do with people suffering from this disorder.

What was Ty to do?

After a long hard look at every option and trying to fix it on her own, she decided to look to Christ. She essentially challenged Christ, "OK, if You truly are the Creator, then who knows better than You how to fix me." So Ty began a journey of studying Who God is, His character, how He works, and what the Bible says about depression. Little did she know at the time God was already working out circumstances and people to come alongside her to help her get into God's Word and study to know Him more.

How can Ty and others like her be free from depression and anxiety?

The answer is Jesus Christ.

In Luke 4:18, Jesus says, "The Spirit of the Lord is on Me, because He has anointed me to proclaim good news to the poor. He has sent me to proclaim freedom for the prisoners and recovery of sight for the blind, to set the oppressed free." Someone suffering from depression and anxiety feels like they are in prison, like they are oppressed. That's why I have named this book *Released* because I know that there is freedom from being oppressed and depressed.

By the way, would you like to know why I know

so much about Ty? The person I have been telling you about is *my* story.

I am Ty (a nickname given to me by my Father.)

I have been free of depression and anxiety for 27 years—100% free, praise God! All the glory goes to God, and I have written this book to show you the things that God showed me as I went through this journey to know Him more.

You see, this life is temporary; eternity is forever. We think of this life as so important, when, in reality, it is but a drop in the scheme of things. In Randy Alcorn's book, *The Treasure Principle*, he put it like this: our life is a dot on a line, and the line is eternity. We live our lives like the dot is the most important part.

The dot: Life on Earth   *The line: Life in Heaven*

Before reading this book: I want you to consider, "Are you living a life where you're in control? Or is God in control?"

Who do you want to have control?

My question is not only who controls your life, but what and who are you living for?

I'll be the first to admit I have lived a lot of my life for myself and really wanted control of it. When I went through depression, I can remember God revealing this to me, and Him speaking to me, "Do you want to control your life? Or do you want Me to? Because if you want Me to, it will mean life. If you want control, go ahead, but it will mean misery and death."

I had heard about Jesus' death, burial, and resurrection a hundred times before, but someone put it to me like this and made it so personal. I never will forget it. I want to give my life to Jesus, and I never want control again. This is how it was explained to me: Jesus loves you so much, He left His royal throne to protect you, to go through the same things you have gone through and will go through, and died for you, because He knew there had to be a payment for sins and that I couldn't pay for them. But the part I love most, that helped me to realize that He loved me so much, is that when He was dying on the Cross, He told the Father to put the sins of the world on Him. When He was on the Cross, He said, "Father, put Tina's sins, and the depression, and anything else in her life, put it on Me. Let Me feel it and suffer it for her, so that she can have freedom from it."

Now I want you to think of Christ on the Cross, and think of Him hanging there, suffering and telling the Father, "Put ___(your name)___'s sins and pain and suffering and depression and bad thoughts and worries and anxieties on me. God, put them on Me. Let Me pay for them, so they can have freedom from this."

Doesn't this make you love God even more? And if you have never done so, don't you want to give

Him your life, because He paid for your sins and your suffering? He did this for you so you could have life and have it more abundant. Do you know anyone who loves you more than this?

You see we know we all sin. The Bible tells us that worry and depression are sins because we are, in essence, saying we don't trust God, and we don't think God is in control; He is not big enough to handle things. The Bible tells us in Romans 3:23, "For all have sinned, and come short of the glory of God."

God knew we couldn't be perfect. That is why He came down to earth to make a way for us to go to heaven, so He could pay for our sins. That is God's mercy to us. He left His throne in glory to come down and live on this earth, and He lived a sinless life so that, when He died on the Cross, He could pay the penalty of our sin. He had no sin, but took ours instead. "All we like sheep have gone astray; we have turned every one to his own way; and the Lord hath laid on Him (Jesus) the iniquity (sin) of us all" (Isaiah 53:6).

Then God rose again on the third day. This is the day we celebrate Easter, because He conquered death. He defeated Satan and death. And so when we die, we can have eternal life with Him.

This makes Christmas and Easter so much more meaningful to those of us who are Christians. You see, if you have never accepted what Christ has done for you, I would like you to consider what He has done. You accept it by faith—not head knowledge, like you would as if it were a historical fact. It is historical fact, but so is Abraham Lincoln as the 16th president. It's not temporary faith, like when you're in big trouble, or in danger, and you cry out to God, "Please help me out of this situation." Then as soon as the situation is over, you are back to controlling your own life.

The way you accept what Christ has done for you is saving faith—trusting Jesus alone for eternal life. Resting on Christ alone and what He has done to pay the price for you, not anything that you have done or can do. Because if it were something you could do, Christ would not have had to die. It would have all been useless. The Bible says, "Trust on the Lord Jesus Christ and you will be saved" (Acts 16:31). Now it says "the Lord Jesus." That means Jesus, Who died for you, but also "Lord," which means turning control of your life over to Him. You can't choose to have Him as Savior so you go to heaven when you die, but not Lord who guides your life. It says "the Lord Jesus Christ."

The only way to have true healing from depression and anxiety is to have Christ as your Lord and Savior. You can have Him as your Lord and Savior right now if you choose. How do you do this?

Transfer your trust from what you have been depending on to get you to heaven—such as being a good person, or good deeds—and trust in what Christ did for you to purchase a place in heaven, by paying for you to enter into heaven with His life. Some people say, "Well that is too easy. I have to do something." But it wasn't easy for Christ when He paid the debt for you.

Accept Christ as Savior. Tell Him you want Him in your life. He tells us in Revelation 3:20, "Behold, I stand at the door, and knock: if any man hear my voice, and open the door, I will come in to him."

Repent: Be willing to give control of your life to Him and quit trying to run your life yourself. Be willing to give up anything that is not pleasing to Him. Will you be able to be perfect after you accept Christ? No. That is why He had to die for us. But your desires will be different. They will not be to do the things you have done before that are displeasing to Him. You may still fall back into your old habits, but your desire will be to put those aside. And then, with His help, you will be able to live a life that is more pleasing to Him.

Go to God in prayer. You can receive His gift of eternal life right now. Romans 10:10–13 says, "For with the heart man believes unto righteousness; and with the mouth confession is made unto salvation. For whosoever shall call upon the Lord shall be saved."

If you want Him as your Lord and Savior, just ask Him right now. What do I say to Him? Just tell

Him you know you are a sinner, you are struggling, and you realize you do not deserve eternal life. But you realize what He did for you in coming down here to live as a man, to experience all that you will experience in your life, and He did it without sinning, and you realize you cannot do that. He knew that and that is why He died for you. Then He defeated Satan over sin, and He defeated death by coming back to life so that you can have victory over sin and death also, but only through Him. Ask Him to forgive you of any sin in your life and to help you to turn away from anything that might not please Him and ask Him to take control of your life. Thank Him for making a way for you to have the gift He bought for you, the gift of eternal life, and also the gift of a Savior Who is there to lead and guide you.

My prayer is that you will make Jesus your Savior before reading this book, or for those who have already accepted Him as your Savior, it will remind you what we have in Christ, and to lean on Him more.

The Bible says in John 6:47, "I say unto you, He that believes in Me has everlasting life."

Praise God.

If you have just asked God into your life, welcome to the family. Today is your spiritual birthday. Celebrate it like you would any other birthday.

May God bless and heal you as you read this book.

CHAPTER 1

Prison

For God is not a God of Disorder but of Peace.

I Corinthians 14:33

I hope that in reading this book you will be encouraged and strengthened through Christ. I also hope that the things I share with you will help you to be an overcomer. The things that I share may seem very simple at first, but when you start putting them into practice, a little at a time, but consistently, you will see all are not so simple, but have a major impact on how you handle life and things in life.

I want you to know the reasons I decided to write this book. One, so you may be spared the imprisonment of depression and anxiety that I went through. You see, I didn't learn all of the things I am going to share with you in this book at once; it was a process. If you could see the steps I learned through many years, and if you could start applying them, I hope to save you many years of heartache. Two, so you know you are not the only one going through this. There are others out there who have been where you are and who are going through the same things you are. I am not a medical doctor, nor am I a psychologist or a psychotherapist, but someone who has experienced anxiety and depression to its fullest and knows how you are feeling. If you are not experiencing this, but you know someone who is, it helps them to know they are not alone, and there are those of us who have gone through what they are going through and have made it. This can give them hope.

And above all, I hope what you learn in this book will help you to depend, cry out to, and love the Lord more intimately than you ever thought possible. As a matter of fact, I have a relationship with my Lord that is so deep because of my experience that I thank Him for allowing me to go through years of depression. I know that sounds strange, and you can't imagine thanking Him for the pain, but you will. And that is my prayer for those of you who read the book—that your relationship with Jesus is one you will never take for granted or ever want to be the same again. After going through anxiety and depression for several years, I can tell you that I am an overcomer through Christ who strengthens me.

I can tell you I was a pro at putting on a false face, making people think I was fine. But inside I was dying and crying for relief. I'm not sure I can even describe what my mind was going through—like I was stuck in a prison and it couldn't get out. It was screaming, "Oh God, help me to get out and not have these thoughts and feelings." But no relief was in sight. Now those who have and are going through this know exactly what I mean, but if you are reading this to understand others, you will grasp some of it, but you cannot fully understand unless you have been there. The best thing you can do to help someone get through is tell the truth. Tell them you don't understand, but you will stand behind them and pray with and for them. There was a time that my husband didn't even know what was going on until one day I reached a breaking point. I couldn't hide it from him any longer. I wanted to hurt my child and didn't know why I was having such ugly thoughts. I even took steps to hurt her, but cried out to the Lord instead and asked Him to help me. It was a true cry of desperation. I knew that there was no other way, unless God intervened, that I was not going to make it out of this alive.

Because of the thoughts I was having, I had decided that if I continued down this path, it would be better for me not to live than to live in prison and live with the thought I had hurt my own child, whom I loved dearly. I loved her so much, but even after my husband knew, I still played the game and hid it from family and friends.

That was just part of my problem. I wasn't sleeping at night. Things are magnified and you panic at night, but I couldn't even get out of bed in the day. I did the bare necessities in life—and when I say bare necessities, I mean the bare necessities. I can remember eating just because I knew I had to stay alive. When I started eating it would make me sick, but I would force myself to eat a few bites. I had to stay alive to take care of my husband and child. That tells you how messed up I was. On one hand I wanted to hurt my child; on the other hand I wanted to protect and care for her. I can remember not showering for days and not doing dishes or cleaning. I couldn't. It was all I could do to function in any way, shape, or form. It took me a long time to admit what was going on inside. I know now it was pride, which the Bible says that God hates. It wasn't until later I was willing to tell people what I had gone through—not just to tell, but to give God glory. I wish I had learned that lesson sooner. I did not realize that in sharing, chains that bind you began to break (more on that later).

You see, at church people thought I was fine, but they didn't know there was a war and a struggle going on inside of me, that I felt I was out of control. I know there are people in church today who are struggling. It may not be depression, as in my case, but they put on a good face. It might be a struggle with sin they are trying to overcome, such as gambling, cheating on a spouse, pornography—anything that is a chain and keeps you defeated.

One key is, we have got to take the focus off ourselves and onto Christ and others, realizing you can't do it. Only Christ can break the chains. There are steps He expects you to take to help yourself, but no matter how hard you try, Christ has to be the One Who works through you. When you give up is when He can begin His work. I know it is hard to do when you feel so overwhelmed, so I am hoping the steps in this book will help you on your journey to knowing and loving Christ more.

I want you to know I understand and know what it is like to feel like you are losing control. I know what it is like to be somewhere and feel like the walls are closing in on you and you have to get out of there and get control, because things are spinning out of control. I know what it is like to have suicidal thoughts, or thoughts of hurting someone you love, and then wonder where in the world those thoughts came from and why you are thinking such things, and, if you're going to think such things, it would be better for you to die than to hurt someone else. I know what it is like to live in fear all the time, yet you can't quite put your finger on what is making you this way. I know what it is like for your heart to start pounding and your head to get light and you're thinking, "What is wrong with me?" I know what it is like to cry and cry, and, when someone asks you what is wrong, you don't know—you don't know what to tell them except you feel like your life is falling apart and you don't know why. I know what it is like when you try to explain these thoughts and feelings to others, and they don't know what you're really going through. Or to think "no one has ever felt the way I am feeling." They say they know what you're feeling, or they try to explain one time how they felt, and you realize they have no clue, so you shut down even more, thinking, "no one has ever had it as bad," and you are never going to get better because there has never been a case this bad and no one will know what to do; you are the worst case ever possible. I know what it is like to feel this way.

I also know that these are all lies from Satan, the enemy, and if we believe these lies and not what God tells us in Scripture, then you truly are defeated.

I may not have listed everything I have ever thought or felt, and I may not have listed what you have ever thought or felt, but I want you to know I have been there. I have had one doctor tell me that I would have been considered manic-depressive, bipolar, and struggled all my life. I also know the world tells us through commercials and advertisements that we are not to ever feel sad or bad, and, if we do, there is something wrong with us. But I also know that there are so many Scriptures in the Bible telling us we are going to have times like these, how to overcome, and that it is OK. Have you ever known anyone who has lived this life without struggles and trials? The answer has to be "no." That is because God tells us we will have them. That is also why He tells us in James 1:2 to "Consider it pure joy, my brothers, whenever you face trials of many kinds. Because you know the testing of your faith develops perseverance."

Perseverance is a quality of spiritual growth, a way of knowing and resting in the fact that Christ will work out situations and you can lean on Him. That is what God wants. He wants you to grow to be more like Him and realize that He is in control of life, yours and all that is around you. When we try to take control, this is when things get crazy.

I was counseling a girl one time with anorexia, and I asked her what made her ever start the eating habits she had developed. She said she was at a time in her life where everything in her life was out of control and that was the one area she could control—what she ate and how she exercised. I pointed out to her, "But don't you see, you are not in control. It has control of your thoughts, your actions, when you do things or don't do things, when you go places and don't go places, when you eat and when you don't eat. Don't you see it is controlling you?"

For the first time someone was straight with her instead of just treating her like a porcelain doll. No one wanted to make her upset, fearful she would sink further into her eating disorder. All she needed was someone to be honest and tell her it is the age-old lie from Satan—that you can have control of your life. When we are going through depression and anxiety, it is because we feel like things are out of control; we want to have control of our own life instead of God.

As we go through this journey together, know that I have prayed for you that God will use this as a step for you to overcome and have victory in Jesus.

I will also share with you in each chapter Scripture that God has so graciously put in His Holy Word, so that we may know how, through Him, to overcome. I will share some practical tips on things you can implement in your life, and, with Christ's help, you can get through this, be victorious, and bring God glory as you share your story with others. I will warn you that as you start to break free, Christ will put others in your life who He wants you to share your story with to help them. Don't be afraid to share what Christ has done for you and how He has set you free. People won't think you are crazy. That is another lie from Satan, and we will talk about that more in depth in a later chapter.

Personal Application

As I began to feel relief from my depression, I realized it was because I had started studying the attributes of God, His character. I had begun studying His Word to get help for my depression; I figured if He created me, then He knows best how to fix me. But it wasn't until I started studying *Him* that I began to have release. What I noticed was I didn't really know God. Well, I didn't know Him well enough to trust Him to let go of my fears and anxieties, even old habits. But once I began to know Him, I began to trust Him and let go of some of my anxieties.

Now when I read God's Word, I ask myself three questions about what I have just read. Here are my questions to myself.

1. What does the passage I am reading tell me about God?
2. What does the passage say in general?
3. What do I do with my life today that helps me apply the passages I have read today?

At the end of each chapter I am going to give you a few verses to look up and help you apply God's truth to your life. There will also be questions to follow and a page for personal reflection. You may also want to keep a journal as you go through the book so you can write down and reflect on what God is doing in your life.

⚷ Passages to Ponder

Psalm 8:4

Psalm 46:1

Psalm 121:3

Isaiah 41:10

Matthew 10:30–31

Luke 12:7

⚷ Practical Application

1. Your depression or difficult situation may bring you into a deeper relationship with Christ and produce greater love, joy, and peace? Do you think this is possible? Do you think it will be worth it?

2. What would look like if you trusted God to free you from depression? Are you allowing yourself the possibility to be free? How does this question make you think differently than what commercials and other media tell us?

3. God holds back the oceans. He makes the sun come up by day and the moon by night. He is controlling all this, yet He cares and knows you so intimately. What does knowing this mean to you and how does it comfort you?

4. God tells us in His Word that He neither slumbers nor sleeps. Does knowing this help you to rest more?

5. Who is your strength, help, and the one who lifts you up? Are you looking to others or trying to provide this for yourself? If so, why? What lies have you believed that makes you look to anything other than Christ?

⚷ Prayer

Write out a prayer asking God to help you know Him more, to seek His presence more, and to grow closer to Him every day. Also ask God to help you give total and complete control of your life to Him.

⚿ Personal Reflections

CHAPTER 2

Preparation

Your word is a lamp to my feet and a light to my path.

Psalm 119:105

How do you prepare to go through depression or anxiety? If you have ever gone through it before and have a hold on it now, hang on, because there may be times when you face it again. But it doesn't have to be depression. It could be anything—changes in life, a child who goes astray, a death of a loved one—any one of these things. You can prepare yourself to handle any situation as it comes your way without coming apart. You do this by studying and knowing Scripture. You say, "Oh, I know that, and I know I should study Scripture." But do you really know why? Let me give you some good reasons why.

When you are going through depression and anxiety, you are being told a bunch of lies from Satan and the world. Satan loves to get at you when you are weak and down. He will choose the times when things aren't right with you. In Matthew 4, you read in verses 2 and 3, that Satan chose what he thought would be a time of weakness. It tells us Jesus had just finished fasting for 40 days and 40 nights. It also says He was hungry. I don't know about you, but when I am hungry and I haven't had food for a while, I am weak. The point being, Satan has a strategic plan to get us while we are down and we have to prepare ourselves for this. Now I know we can't always blame Satan for all our trials; sometimes we bring it upon ourselves, allowing ourselves to get in such a weak condition by not eating, sleeping, or staying in God's Word like we should. But Satan also tries to creep in, and when you believe his lies, you are putting him on the throne of your life and taking Christ off the throne.

Jesus gives us a great example of what to do when being tempted by Satan in the Garden, where Jesus was praying. He quotes Scripture to Satan. Listen to the sequence of events here in Matthew 4:1–3. Satan

whispers lies to Jesus, telling Him, "If you are the
Son of God, make the stones become bread." First
of all, Satan is questioning God and His power. Isn't
that what Satan does to us also? He tries to make
us question God's power and provision, as far as
our healing is concerned. We feel like we will never
be the same again. (And by the way, when you get
through the depression, you will be thanking God
that you are not the same person you were before.)
Second, Satan is reminding Jesus that He is hungry.
Satan does the same thing to us—always reminding
us what the problem is. Here it is hunger, but it might
be something like this for us: "You are always going
to be plagued with this depression." Or have you
ever thought this? "People won't like you if you tell
them what you're dealing with. They will think you're
crazy, so you must be." All lies from Satan. He is the
master of hitting you while you are down. So we have
to use Jesus as our example.

Jesus quotes Scripture in verse 4, then in verses
5–6. Again we see Satan attempting to tempt Jesus
again by telling Him, "Go ahead, throw yourself
down." Then Satan tries to use Scripture, out of
context, and tells Jesus, "The Scripture says that
the angels will support you and you will not hurt
yourself." I see Satan trying the same lies on those
with severe depression. "Go ahead and kill yourself. If
your God is really God, He will save you and protect

you, or you will be better off dead because you will be with Jesus." We will be happy when we are there with our Heavenly Father, but it is not for us to decide when, where, and how we go to be with Him. You may very well be going through this so that you can help others. Either way, don't listen to Satan's lies. But if you notice, Jesus once again quotes Scripture in verse 7 and tells Satan "Do not test the Lord your God." Do you see, in order to fight the enemy, you have to know Scripture to fight back?

Again, in verse 8 and 9, Satan doesn't give up, so we don't need to give up either. We have to keep running to our Savior over and over, looking in and to His Word to know how to fight. This time, Satan tempts Jesus with worldly possessions, as if Jesus doesn't already own them. Satan and our fleshly desires temps us the same way. Satan says, "Follow me, and I will give you all these things you want." And our flesh says, "If you have just this one more thing, it will make you happy." So we fill our lives trying to buy things that make us feel good for the moment and then wear off. You have to keep buying and keep buying, and you quickly realize things are not keeping you happy. That is because our only source of joy will only come from Christ and Christ alone.

After Satan tempts Jesus with the kingdoms and worldly pleasures, Jesus quotes Scripture in verse 10 and simply tells Satan to go away. Then He tells us to "worship the Lord your God and serve only Him." That is where you are going to find your peace again. This tells me that Jesus was giving us an example of what to do. When tempted to believe lies from Satan or lies from our flesh, we are to know Scripture well enough that we can quote it and have it ready for our defense. If Jesus quoted Scripture to fight off Satan, then we, who are much weaker than Jesus, have to be able to do the same.

Some of the biggest lies that Satan tries to fill our minds with when going through depression and anxiety are, "You are not good enough...you will never be good enough...you are crazy...there will never be help for you...you are going to live like this all your life...you might as well take your life so you won't have to deal with this anymore." One reason Satan would love for us to believe these lies is because, if we do, we will be defeated, and we will not be a good representation of Christ. If we do not overcome, we will not be able to help others to overcome and help those who are not children of Christ. You see, if non-Christians are seeing Christians overcoming depression and anxiety, they are going to want what we have, which is Christ in our lives.

I love Ephesians 6:11. God tells us to put on the full armor of God so that we can stand against the tactics of the devil. And then it goes on to say in verse 14–17 to put on the belt of truth, the breastplate of righteousness, the shield of faith, helmet of salvation and, I love this part, the sword of the spirit, which is the Word of God. You see, each item God mentions is an item of protection, except one—the sword of faith. This is an offensive weapon, something to fight back with. You can protect yourself all day long from the enemy, but if you don't have something to fight back with, you will always by running for protection instead of defeating and conquering. Eventually, the enemy will overtake you.

Now another thing I want to point out to you about studying Scripture and spending time in God's Word is that this is how God speaks to you. How do you know what He wants to share with you, or how He wants to comfort you, and how you can act and react when facing the struggles in your life, if you are not giving God the time to talk to you? You wouldn't build a house without speaking to a contractor and seeing what he can do, what his specialty is. So we shouldn't try to build this temple of the Lord's, which is our body, soul, and mind, without asking Him and seeing what He has to say about what He wants and expects, and how He would like for it to be built. How can we better construct this temple for the glory of God? How better to know the right way to build up this temple, than to ask the Creator of this temple Who knows it better than we do and knows the best way to build and to grow.

Often times with depression and anxiety, I would have doubts of my salvation. I was always feeling that there was no way I could be saved and have these thoughts and feelings—always feeling defeated or having evil thoughts against others. But when I started getting into God's Word faithfully, not just a quick little devotion a day but reading it, asking questions about what it is saying to me, and applying it to my life, that is when I realized that the doubts of salvation went away, along with a lot of other lies Satan was trying to use to defeat me. Our former pastor, Adrian Rogers, used to say, "Don't worry about what you don't understand when you read the Bible. There will be enough of what you do understand that if you begin to apply what you do understand, then the things you don't understand will start to make more sense." There will be plenty you do understand, and if you take those things and apply them to your life, and if you are obedient to what God is showing you to help you, then you will begin thinking on the right things and see the joy and peace come back into your life.

Don't think you are going to get a quick fix. That is what the world tells you should happen, but God is more loving than that. He knows it is part of the spiritual growth process. To know and to love Him more comes with time. The world tells you if you feel this way, it is wrong, and you need immediate relief. It does feel like that at times (more on that later). Being in the Word also helps because of the power, which is Jesus Christ. "In the beginning was the word and the word was with God and the Word was God" (I John 1:1).

Let me give you another benefit of being in God's Word. You handle situations differently. I know I do. I don't get overwhelmed as easily, angry as easily, or frustrated. You react differently towards people, especially family members—children or your spouse, for example. If you show me someone who is being treated unfairly, and they react with kindness, I will show you a person in God's Word. A person whose life is spinning out of their control, through circumstances beyond their control, yet they still give God glory, they seem at rest and take things as they come—I will show you a person in God's Word. I want to be that person, don't you?

The other type person is overwhelmed, depressed, and can't see a way out. A "woe is me" complex and can't look past themselves. I know. I have been there, and I really don't want to go back.

Being in God's Word builds your faith. In Romans 10:17, the Bible tells us that faith comes by hearing, the hearing of the Word of God, and in Isaiah 55:11 it tells us that His Word will not go void. In other words, when you are in Scripture, it will be useful to you and help you defeat the enemy.

So if you are going through depression, anxiety, or panic attacks, the first thing I would tell you is get in God's Word immediately. When I was going through this, I would sit up for hours and hours and read my Bible. To this day, I could not tell you what I read at that time, but there was a peace and comfort that I couldn't explain. I was so out of it, I don't think I could even comprehend the power that was there, but I know one thing—it gave me comfort and peace when I couldn't find it anywhere else or with anyone else. God's Word helps us to overcome through Christ.

I think as Christians, the Spirit is not going to leave you alone until you get in His Word because He wants to speak to you. So, He will do what it takes to bring you to Him, even allow us to go through depression and anxiety. I truly believe that is what He did in my life. He knew what my breaking point was, and He was willing to watch me go through pain in order to have a wonderful relationship with me. It's just like those of us who are parents who have a child who needs stitches. They scream and cry and do not want the doctor to touch them. You have to hold them down and watch them go through pain, because you know the outcome is what is best for them.

That is the same with our Heavenly Father. He knows the outcome and what is best for us. We are

God's children; what a loving Heavenly Father we have. He is willing to watch us and help us go through the pain, knowing that the outcome is a much better place to be than to stay where we are at.

The one thing I tell people who tell me what they are going through is that one day you will be thankful for this trial. I get one of three reactions. They look as if I am crazy, and they are not sure they ever want to talk to me again. Or they don't look at me as if I am crazy, they just tell me they think I am. Then I have those who can't imagine ever being thankful for this, but I trust you and look forward to that day. I can tell you I have shared with many people, and, when I see they have come through to the other side, I ask them what God showed them through all this. It is always the same: "I can't believe God loved me this much to allow me to go through this, and, without Him, I could have never made it. I am so thankful because I have a relationship with Him. I have never had a closeness and intimacy before with Christ, and the knowledge that God and I can get through anything together." You feel like you have a closeness with God that no one else has. It is just between you and God, because He was with you all the time, holding your hand, walking with you, sometimes just sitting while He comforted you, wrapping you in protection and love, when you didn't even realize it. At the time, you don't feel it. As a matter of fact, you wonder where

He is when you are going through it. But on the other side, what sweet fellowship! After you come through, you can look back and see the guidance, protection, and comfort.

Another really good reason for studying God's Word (can you tell I really feel strongly about God's Word?) is that it tells us in Psalm 119:105, "Thy word is a lamp unto my feet and a light unto my path." Many of us know that Scripture by heart, but have you taken the time to consider what the writer of that psalm was saying when He made this statement? Let's break it down for a moment.

The Word of God is a lamp unto my feet. Have you ever gotten up in the middle of the night and stubbed your toe on something because you couldn't see what was on the floor? If you had just had a little lamp, even the smallest night light, it would have helped you to see what you were about to step on. Well, it's the same with God's Word. It helps you to see what you are going to face, and helps you not to step on something and hurt yourself. Then the Scripture goes on to say "a light unto my path." If you are carrying the light with you as you go along the way, it continues to keep you from running into things that might hurt you. In other words, if you carry that light with you in the middle of the night to go through your house, you can see not just what is immediately in front of you, but what lies ahead and

how to work your way around it and not get hurt. If
you are in a strange place you have never been before,
and it is dark, the light not only lets you see where you
are, but also which way to go. Say there is a wall, the
light would show you not to go that way—it would
be a dead end. But the light also reveals to you there
is a door and a way out. (Jesus is that door for us.)
Without the light, you would not have known there
was a door. In trials and struggles you may have
never been through before, if you are carrying God's
Word with you in your heart and mind, you will be
aware of snares that are waiting around the corner,
and you will be prepared to avoid them—things such
as temptations, and thoughts and lies that flood your
mind. You will be able to apply Scripture to them and
bind them in the name of Christ. You will be able to
find your way out. You will also be able to recognize,
right off, that it is a lie from the enemy and stop it in
its tracks.

A great example is when we get the case of, what
I like to call, the "I deserve." You know, the "I deserve
this or that" or "I worked really hard for this, and I
should be able to do it or buy that and no one can tell
me otherwise." Well, that is a big indication that you
are justifying something that is not from God, but
from the enemy, and you should be able to take those
thoughts captive.

Psalm 119:11 tells us to hide/treasure God's Word in our hearts so that we might not sin against God. I love Hebrews 4:12; it tells us that "the word of God is living and active. Sharper than any double edged sword, it penetrates/pierces even to dividing soul and spirit, joints and marrow; it judges the thoughts and attitudes of the heart."

We tend to make this Christian life harder than it is. We think we have to keep our thoughts and mind in check, when it says in this Scripture that if we are in God's Word, He will keep our thoughts and attitudes in check. So, either we don't realize the power of God's Word, we don't study and apply, or we don't want to be convicted. This is a great question to ask yourself. Which is it with you?

Let me give you some practical ways that have helped me to stay in God's Word.

Get yourself in a weekly Bible study—not just church service, where all you have to do is show up and listen to what God has shown your pastor. But one where you have to do a little homework yourself, something to make you think, dig and apply things to your own life. Somewhere that you will be held accountable if you don't show up. Somewhere you will be missed and called. You will go when you are missed, or you will go because you don't want them bothering you about not coming. We don't always do things for the right reasons. In a perfect world, we would, but I have been in that situation. I have shown up to Bible study only because I was expected to be there, not because of the blessing I would receive, not because it was a time set aside where I could worship the Lord. God has used those times to fill my heart to the brim, humbling me, and helping me to realize He has my best interests at heart. Here I was grumbling; I didn't want to go. Sometimes that is when I get the biggest blessing.

Another way is put Scripture on your dashboard. We spend a lot of times in our cars. Every time you are at a stoplight, you can read over the Scripture and start to memorize it, hiding God's Word in your heart. On your bathroom mirror—we all look in the mirror at least twice a day, in the morning when we are getting ready for the day and at night when we brush our teeth before bed. If we are honest with ourselves, we probably look in that mirror more than twice a day, and it is a great opportunity to look over Scripture.

One thing that I find is that whatever Scripture I am studying, at any given time, God uses throughout the day. Someone will have a need or a hurt and the exact Scripture you are studying is exactly the one they need and, because you have just looked over it, you are able to quote it and reference where it is found. I used to see people who always had the right Scripture at the right time and I thought they were walking Bibles. I felt ashamed I didn't know Scripture as well or as quickly as they did. But now I see that when I am in the Word, whatever I am studying, God uses the Scriptures. Whenever someone would quote Scripture to me, I would say, "How did you know that right Scripture to tell me?" More times than not, it happened to be a passage in Scripture they happened to be studying at that time. I love it when this happens, because it is my way of knowing God is orchestrating my life with others, to help one another in love. There are those who know an abundance of Scripture off the top of their head. I am not, however, one of them. I can quote a lot of Scripture, but I can't always tell you were it is located. I know the gist of the Scripture, but not the exact words. Of course, there are those that I use quite often that I know well, but not as many as I would like there to be.

Now, one last thing I think will help you to study God's Word and stay in it is to find an accountability person—one who is willing to ask if you have been in God's Word, and not just take a yes for an answer, but ask you about it. Tell them what God has been showing you. That way, you are not just reading Scripture to fill a quota, but you have to ask yourself questions, sometimes looking further to find answers. You will be more consistent if you know you are going to have someone ask you about it. Before you know it, it becomes a habit for you, and if you find yourself missing a day, you wonder what God had to share with you that you skipped. You miss time with God. Be sure not to just pick someone for an accountability partner that you think will be good, but pray that God will send this person to you because He knows the one who will be able to give you the time and encouragement you need.

One of the first things I do, if I am going to counsel or disciple someone, is to get them in a Bible study and have them do some daily work. I will call them and have them tell me what they are learning. You will be amazed at how quick of a difference this makes in your life. I have even had one girl who has been on medication since she was 13, and now in her early 30s, say she had never felt this good in her life. The medication helped her not to have the anxiety and depression, but it did not help her have joy and peace. The only change she had made was to get in God's Word consistently and be accountable.

Q Passages to Ponder

II Samuel 22:11

Psalm 19:7–14

John 17:17

Jeremiah 29:13

Psalm 34:4

Proverbs 8:17

Proverbs 2:6

I Chronicles 28:9

Hebrews 11:6

Q Practical Application

1. Make a list of all the attributes of God from
   II Samuel 22:24 and Psalm 19:7–14. ~ Blameless;
   ~ Perfect; ~ Trustworthy; ~ Right; ~ Radiant;
   ~ Pure; ~ Firm/Sure; ~ Sweet like honey

2. Many of the above Passages to Ponder underscore
   the importance of being in God's Word. Why is it
   so necessary to be in God's Word and how does it
   affect your life?

3. When you look at the attributes of God, how does it help you to rely on Him?

Reinforces the fact that He is a sure thing, that He is perfect & can be trusted always.

4. How does what you learned about God in this chapter help you to see your current circumstances differently?

Reminds me that I don't need to rely on my finite strength, but to put all my weight on his infinite love, strength & care.

5. How does knowing God more affect your future, and how will it affect the way you study Him in the future?

⚘ Prayer

Write out a prayer asking for help to seek Him more, know Him more intimately, and to be more consistent in your walk with Him.

⚷ Personal Reflections

58 RELEASED

faith! I know that, s
Scripture and
Christian
given
S

Prayer

Call upon me in the day of trouble; I will deliver you, and you will honor me.

Psalm 50:15

I think that it is great how God gives us Scripture to tell us what to do and then He gives us the result. If we pray to Him in our times of trouble, the result will be deliverance. Then, who will get the glory? It will be Almighty God, Who is the One Who delivered you.

Prayer—what a big essential for the Christian

far, I have suggested reading
prayer, the two very basics of the
faith, but hopefully, I have shown and
you different thoughts and ideas on studying
Scripture, and hopefully, I will be able to give you
different thoughts and ideas about prayer, maybe
some nuggets you haven't thought of before, or maybe
just a reminder on how to pray, when to pray, and the
importance of prayer.

You wouldn't like a relationship where you were
the only one talking, and the other person never talked
to you. Nor would you like a relationship where the
other person was talking, and you never got to say a
word.

Reading Scripture is God's way of speaking to us,
as well as through His Spirit in us. Prayer is our way
of talking to Him. That's two-way communication.
Here are ways I want you to consider praying, to help
you not only get through depression and anxiety, but
to thrive through it. The ultimate goal is to give God
glory.

Let's think about praying in these ways. To...

- Rely
- Reveal
- Revive
- Renew
- Remember

Now let me explain each step a little further.

Rely

We have to pray and ask God to help us to rely on Him. It is not our nature to do it this way. If we were really truthful with ourselves, a lot of times we get into—whether thrown in or go into—situations where we start trying to take care of ourselves, instead of going to God right off and relying on Him to lead, guide, and direct us in the paths we need to pursue to take care of any given situation. Let me ask you a question. When we get into an argument with our spouse or a confrontation with our children, do we rely on the Lord to give us the way to handle the situation or do we go into the conversation on our own and then ask later for help? Most of us go right into it before taking it to the Lord and asking for his help to deal with a situation.

I was challenged with this at one point: to go to God before going to a person to ask them about something that they might not like, or asking God when you have had a disagreement with someone. So I tried it and it worked. The situation always turned out better because I was going in with God's, not my agenda. Now I will warn you, sometimes when I pray about a situation concerning my husband or children, sometimes God convicts me that it is not a concern of mine, or I am trying to handle a situation that is not mine to handle, but His to handle and His alone. I

am not to help Him. It always shocks me that I didn't
see it that way before, but in any case it still turns
out better because I had myself all worked up over
something I shouldn't have. God had it under control
all along.

Going to God in prayer, even over the little things
in life, cuts out a lot of the anxiety, because we realize
it is in God's control, not ours. Now it will take some
practice to remind yourself to take any situation to
God first before approaching it yourself, but once you
start, it becomes much easier. I will say, the longer I
am a Christian and the more I am in God's Word, it
occurs to me to take any and every situation to Him
immediately. I hate to tell you that during my worst
hours of depression and panic were when I cried out
to Him in desperation—when I had no other choice
but to rely on God—I wish I could say that was the
first thing I always did. Unfortunately, it is not always
the first thing I do. There are and were times I search
for help from medical experts, friends, or pastors
before I sought out God. Looking back now, I see there
is nothing wrong with seeking medical help, seeking
guidance from family, friends, and pastors. But if
I had sought the Lord first, I know He would have
guided me to the right people and places. It would
have brought Him glory first and helped a lot quicker
than it did with me trying to solve problems myself,
trying to figure out what was wrong with me on my

own, without even asking the Creator Who created me. Who knows better how to fix someone than the one who made them? Very simple I know, but very profound.

Reveal

We want to also ask God to reveal anything that He wants you to learn while going through this experience. It might be lessons He wants you to learn; it might be things in your life He is wanting you to change that He has been convicting you about, but you haven't been willing to change. Here's an example from my life: at one point, God had convicted me about watching too much television and wasting time. (It could be any number of things, such as hanging around someone who is influencing you in the ways of the world. It could be gossip, adultery, lying, cheating, or stealing. You know what it is that God speaks to you about.) Wasting time happened to be something God was working on my heart about. It may be something totally different with you. It may be a bad habit, a way of living that is dishonoring to Him—I don't know, but ask Him to reveal it to you so you can be aware of it. Then you will have to ask Him to help you to rely on Him and to help you overcome whatever it is Christ is working on in your heart. Sometimes, God will allow discomfort, such as depression in your life, as a wake-up call to listen to

Him and recognize what area of your life He wants to change and grow in you.

Then you want to ask Him to…

Revive

You want to ask Him to revive you and give you strength to get through this time of struggle and turmoil. And believe me, if you are going through depression, you know you feel like you are in a total state of turmoil. Also ask Him to revive you so that you will have the strength to portray Him and proclaim Him during this time, always giving Him glory. Then ask God to give you the strength to come to Him always—the strength to carry out any act of obedience that might be involved, because when God asks us to give up something to Him, it isn't always going to be easy. Most of the time it is not easy; that way we have to rely on Him in order for God to be glorified in the end.

Another way to pray is to pray that God will…

Renew

Psalm 51:10 says, "Create in me a clean heart, O God, and renew a steadfast spirit within me." I love this Scripture because when David wrote this Psalm, he had realized what a sinful state in which he had been living. And so, when he writes this to God, you can see the example he is to us.

First, he asked God to create in him a clean heart—a heart that desires the things and ways of God. A clean heart, one that sees things from God's perspective, not our own. A clean heart, not the one he had at that point. And we need that, too. He was asking God to help him see things the way God sees them and not to have the desire of sin. We need that, too.

Then you see David is desperate; He cries out, "O GOD." Now, I don't know if you have yet reached this point, but you do get to a point where all you can do is cry out to God in desperation. You cry out, "O GOD help me," which is where God wants you in the first place, totally relying on Him. Oh, if we could only learn to do that as a first response, instead of as a last resort!

And then one last way to pray is to...

Remember

Remember others in order to take the focus off ourselves. When we are thinking of others, we are not so overwhelmed with feelings about ourselves. Our anxiety and depression seems so much less. One reason you have to pray and ask God to help you to remember others is when you are going through depression and anxiety, it is all you can do to think of anything other than the overwhelming feelings of what you are going through, so you have to ask God to help you renew your mind. Now this may sound simple, but it is not when you are going through depression. When you are constantly thinking of yourself, you are putting yourself in control of your life and are so self-absorbed. Others see it, but you cannot see it. The most loving thing someone said to me was, "It's not all about you." That was really hard for me to hear, but it was true. I was making everything in life and this world about me and it was not at all. People try not to ruffle the feathers of those going through depression and anxiety, when the most loving thing they could do is tell the truth in love. So, be bold. Those who were willing to be truthful to me are the ones who helped me the most. Did I always take it well? NO. Let me say again, NO. As a matter of fact, I would pout and get angry and use it as an excuse to dwell on me again. But it did give me something to think on. Two of the most helpful things to me were to remember that, one, it is not all about me, and, two, that I was not crazy, but my thoughts were. It helped me to separate the two—a bold statement that the thoughts I was having were crazy, and I needed help.

Remembering others also helps you to see where others need help and gives you something else to focus on. When your focus is always on yourself, it builds and seems to multiply. So, ask God to help you to remember others. Philippians 2:4–5 says, "Do not merely look out for your own personal interest, but also for the interest of others. Have this attitude in yourselves which was also in Christ Jesus."

You see, the Bible is telling us that the attitude of Christ Jesus was to think of others. We know this because God was thinking of us when He left His Heavenly home, His throne, His crown, His glory, to come here in this corrupted world so that He could die for us and purchase a place for us in heaven, and so He could share His riches with us. We need to be like-minded with Christ and think of others first. Before going into depression, I was always thinking of others before myself and my family. Needless to say, this was driving my husband crazy. He said I would give away my house, if I could, if someone needed it more than I did, but there has to be a balance. That I had not learned yet. But once I started the downward spiral of depression, all I could do was think of myself. Nothing or no one else mattered.

Ask God to show you who to pray for, who needs it at that time, because if you are going through struggles there are others who are going through tough times, also. Ask Him who might need a note of encouragement, a meal, a personal touch, a phone call. If you are doing things for others it helps take the focus off yourself.

I can remember a time during my depression, and I was learning to put into practice the power of prayer.

I had prayed for God to help me remember others. It was a Wednesday night at prayer meeting and the Lord brought to mind an old Sunday school teacher that I hadn't seen in about six years. I knew she had battled cancer, but the last I had heard she was cancer free. God was about to show me something about His love and care for his children that I will never forget. He brought this lady to my mind, and I had the overwhelming sensation to pray for her family. I turned to my husband and told him I felt like God was telling me to pray for this family, not her, but the family. So we did, not knowing why. The very next morning my sister called and asked if I had heard that Miss Joyce had died the evening before. I asked her what time she had passed away, and it was the same time that I felt like God was telling me to pray for the family. You see, she was in heaven. The family was in need of comfort. I will never forget that because God was showing me several things—that He cares for His children over time and space. They were in another state at the time. He was showing me He knew what I was going through, and He was watching over me. He was showing me He sees everything and was revealing to me He cared. He was showing me there were others in His kingdom, that He would lay me on their hearts to pray for. He was showing me His love was real. I can say this instance was one of the things that helped to bring me out of my constant state of depression. He is God over time and space, Almighty, who is looking down on His children to provide love and comfort. Let God handle your burdens and see if you can help someone else with their burdens. Galatians 6:2 says we are to bare one another's burdens.

In Psalms 55:22, the Bible says to cast your burden upon the Lord, and He will sustain you. He will never allow the righteous to be shaken. Isn't that comforting to know that we can remember others because God is going to take care of all our cares and troubles? And not only take care of them, but it says He will not let us fall. If you are a child of God's, you are one of the righteous, not because of acts that you have done but because of the sacrificial act that He did—to become your sin substitute. You are considered righteous (more about that later). We may not feel it at times, but when you come through the other side, you will see His guidance and protection. Then, don't forget to share with others what God has done for you. Even if you are going through depression and anxiety, dwell on what God has already done for you, how He has brought you through thus far, and ask Him to help you remember those things so that you don't take His grace and mercy for granted. Don't ask, "Why me?" but ask, "What is it, Lord, that you need to show me?"

In Philippians 4:6–7, the Bible tells us, "Do not be anxious about anything, but in everything, by prayer and petition, with thanksgiving, present your requests to God. And the peace of God, which transcends all understanding, will guard your hearts and minds in Christ Jesus." Christ Jesus the Creator, the Almighty God, The Holy One will guard ___(your name)___'s heart and mind. That is an awesome thought.

After talking to God, and covering all the areas I have just shared with you, you also have to take time to listen to what God is telling you. It has to be a two-way conversation. You can talk to God anytime, anywhere, and any place, but you also have to take time to listen. When you accept Christ as your Lord and Savior, the Holy Spirit comes to live inside of you. He wants to speak to you, but you have to let Him. I like to stop in the middle of a prayer time and just see what the Spirit is telling me. Or pause during reading the Bible, and see what He is showing me.

⚘ Passages to Ponder

Lamentations 3:55–59

Hebrews 4:15–16

Romans 8:26

⚘ Practical Application

1. Make a list from the Lamentations passage of what you learned about prayer.

2. What do the verses in Hebrew tell you about how to approach God, and how does that make you pray differently?

3. What does Romans 8:26 tell us about how God knows you and cares for you?

4. What do the above verses tell you about God's intimacy with us?

5. How does seeing His care and intimacy with you change your reliance on the Lord?

🔑 Prayer

Write out a prayer asking God to help you first know His presence before His provision. Tell God your desire to know Him more intimately and to help you to sense His presence each day.

⚷ Personal Reflections

CHAPTER 4

Peace

Behold, how happy is the man whom God reproves, So do not despise the discipline of the Almighty.

Job 5:17

How to make peace, simply stated: Obedience.
We have to face it that all children, at some time or another, have to be disciplined. Even you and I have had to be disciplined, whether from our earthly parents or our Heavenly Father. With discipline there comes a choice: obedience or disobedience.

You can choose. So if you are going through depression or anxiety, ask yourself, "Is this a result of disobedience?" It may or may not be, but it is a good checkup. There is no better feeling than knowing you are right with the Lord, and you can stand clean. In Proverbs 3:11–12, it says, "My son do not despise the Lord's discipline and do not resent his rebuke, because the Lord disciplines those He loves as a father the son He delights in."

I love this because if you realize the Father is disciplining you, then there is security in that. He loves you enough to take the time to discipline you, and there's security in knowing you are one of His children.

One of the results that I suffered during my years of depression and anxiety was doubt of my salvation. At the time, I was too spiritually immature to know that the discipline of the Father is a good thing. All I could say was, "Why is this happening to me?" I can tell you that as a result, I no longer have doubts of my salvation; I do not doubt His love for me. It also encourages me to do spiritual check-ups, such as I mentioned earlier. Any number of things could draw my attention away from the Lord and onto self. I had allowed others to become more important to me than Christ. What He began to show me was that I wanted to control my life and not let Him. I didn't even consider Him in many decisions. The result was depression and thoughts of suicide. He was using this time as a time to discipline me. In the process, God revealed to me that if I wanted to have control of my life I could, but it would ultimately lead to death. If I would let Him have control, then I was choosing life— not just physical life, but abundant life and eternal life. You see, I wanted a Savior to save me from an eternity in hell. Acts 16:31 says, "Believe on the Lord Jesus and you will be saved." Oh, I wanted Jesus, but I did not want that "Lord" part. That meant that the decisions in my life had to be based on God and His Word. God would convict me when I was not doing the right thing. It was much easier when I lead my own life and didn't have to deal with conviction. That is what I thought anyway. What I didn't realize is that my Heavenly Father is too loving to let me keep going down that path. He had to allow things to come in my life where the only choice was to fall on my face before Him. I am convinced if we fall on our faces on a regular basis, then we would not have to be brought to our knees in desperation. But when we are brought to our knees in desperation, it makes us love the Lord so much more intimately because we are so thankful He is there, and we have somewhere to run and hide and rest...when it feels like life is hopeless.

When I was trying to control my life, I was not successful. I was always struggling with thoughts of suicide and hurting others, which would have led me down a road of destruction, prison, or a mental hospital for life. Praise be to God that He revealed this to me, and I was able to choose Him to control my life. Now do I always run to Him immediately? Not always. I am still learning to turn over complete control to Him. I don't know why it is that we go head first in leading our lives, or make quick decisions, or go about our days without first consulting Jesus, and then have to go back and repent and ask for help. I hope that asking for God to take control immediately will become a routine practice in your life. And you will save yourself many days of struggles and trials and discipline. But remember to be thankful that we have a Heavenly Father who loves us enough, is willing to watch us hurt, and takes the time to discipline us, knowing that the result is for our best interest. I have shared some difficult times in my life that God has had to deal with me on, but you may have other areas in your life that God is working on with you. You know what it is in your life. Perhaps when I mentioned things the Lord had to teach me, something came to your mind that the Lord wants you to do, or stop doing, or change. Give to the Lord. It is also encouraging that the Spirit, Who lives in us, will not leave us alone whatever the issues are. Once you give it to God, don't take it back. I didn't say this would be easy. Remember you can't do it alone without God's help. He died that we might have life in

Him and have life more abundantly (John 10:10).

You might ask, "How am I going to know what God is telling me to work on in my life?" Simply by spending time in His Word and in prayer. The world and the enemy are fighting for your mind and desires, so stay in touch with God and be obedient to what it is He is telling you. I love Philippians 4:8. It tells us that, "Whatever is true, whatever is noble, whatever is right, whatever is pure, whatever is lovely, whatever is admirable if anything excellent or praiseworthy think about such things." This Scripture is my test to know if something is actually the world trying to pull me away from God. It also helped me to take the false thoughts and feelings into captivity and turn them over to the Lord, releasing them to Him so that I don't have to take care of them.

When I was going through depression, I had to quit listening to the news broadcast, all together, because of the fear it placed in my heart and mind. I was leaving God out of areas in my life, forgetting no matter what takes place in this world, God is still in control. By listening to the news broadcast, I would get so caught up in the things of the world and would panic that these things would overtake me. I was taking God off the throne—not just the throne of my life, but off the throne of the universe. I had become like a person who did not believe there was a God.

There will be times when you have to give

something up. God may be telling you to give it up sometimes, until you can step back and see what is causing your fear and turmoil. Or sometimes He will call you to give up something altogether, forever. I can now watch the news without fear. When I have the time to watch, it now prompts me to pray for the different situations. By doing so, I am saying, "God, I know You know what is going on in this world, and I am trusting You to take control of the things I have no control over. I trust You to help me carry out the things I can do something about." But you have to let God have control and you let go. You will fail from time to time. You might fail many times, just like a diet, but just because you fail doesn't mean it doesn't work. You had a set-back. Start again fresh and new, not the next day, but the next moment. Keep giving control back to God each time you fail, and, before you know it, it will become automatic and easier. When you completely give it over to Him and realize how freeing it is to let Him have control—the decisions are His to make—you won't want whatever it was you were trying to control.

There are going to be times when it will be hard to face things head on, but listen to this passage in Isaiah 41:10… "So do not fear, __(your name)__, for I am with you; __(your name)__ do not be dismayed, for I am your God. __(your name)__ I will strengthen you; __(your name)__ I will uphold you __(your name)__

with my righteous right hand." This is not just some
Scripture that sounds good, but this is a promise
from God to you. I love inserting my name into this
Scripture because it makes it so personal—not just
talking to someone out there, but to me. You are not in
this alone. God, the King of the Universe, who holds
everything in His hand, is in this with you. What an
incredible thought!

⚡ Passages to Ponder

John 14:26–27

Ephesians 2:14

John 16:7

Psalm 121:2–4

Philippians 4:6–8

⚡ Practical Application

1. What did you learn from the above passages about Who is the giver of Peace?

2. What does the Scripture say about help and where does the help come from?

3. God not only gives peace but peace that surpasses our understanding. This truth is comforting because it tells me that it is not something that is up to me to come up with. How does this bring comfort to you?

4. In Philippians 4:8 God gives us a formula for how to attain His peace. How can you apply this when you are feeling discouraged?

5. How does it bring you peace to know that God does not slumber nor sleep? (Psalm 121:2–4)

⚿ Prayer

Write out a prayer asking God to provide the peace that only He can bring and for His help to rely on Him.

🔑 Personal Reflections

CHAPTER 5

Praise

Because your lovingkindness is better than life, My lips will praise Thee.

Psalm 63:3

You may say that praise is easy, but it really isn't as easy as you think. Or you might say that it is not an essential part of getting over depression. Or that is the last thing you feel like doing, or even thinking about when you are depressed. Because when you are praising you are not depressed. It is not as easy as it sounds. The next time you are really going through a trial, try praising. It is not a natural thing to do when you are hurting and confused, and you feel like you are alone. I'll give you an example. Upon moving to a new city, I found things going wrong all around me. My husband had stayed back to finish out one week of work, and our children had stayed with grandparents for the week, so I could go ahead, unpack the house, and have things ready for the family when everyone arrived to the new town one week later. During that week, in a strange town with no one I knew, everything went wrong. The job I had been told I had was no longer available to me. The house we had rented, in which I had unpacked almost everything, was covered in fleas. I learned this, having woken up with over 100 bites on each leg one morning. I had to pack everything back up so the exterminator could come and spray the house and yard. The boxes I packed up and had stacked on the floor were ruined when I woke up the next morning as it had rained all night and the whole house flooded up to my ankles. Then I tripped on a curtain rod and cut my toe. I used a whole role of paper towels to stop the bleeding. I didn't know there was a hospital not far from me. I was in a new city, didn't know anyone to call, so I just made do. It all seems so comical now, but at the time it was very upsetting. You see, we were moving so my husband could attend seminary and begin working in the ministry. Looking back, I see where Satan was trying to discourage us from moving there, but God was testing us to see if we were faithful to the call. It would have been very easy to call my husband and say the job didn't work out, I hate it here, don't leave your job, and let's not pursue this ministry idea. But I didn't do that. I called my husband to tell him what all had happened in three days time, and all He could say is, "You have to praise the Lord."

I was not happy with that response. I wanted sympathy and caring, and He expects me to praise the Lord when everything under the sun has just gone wrong? After all, I had just faced this all by myself, with no help from him, and He wants me to praise the Lord! You need to know that I was not very kind to my husband on that phone conversation. It was all his fault we were moving anyway. I was happy where I was, and now He is telling me to praise. He must be the crazy one, not me.

As you can tell by this time, I was beginning to question our move into ministry. I was ready to give in and give up. When I got off the phone with him, I was fuming. But since I didn't have anyone to fume to, I just had to tell the Lord about what my husband had to say about the situation, and how out of touch He was with me. In that still small voice I hear, "Praise Me."

"But Lord, did you not hear? Do you not know

what I have been through these last few days?"

"Praise me!"

"But God, you are everywhere. You have seen how I have been treated and what has happened to me."

"Praise Me!"

"But Lord!"

"Praise Me!"

What was a girl to do but start singing praise songs? I must admit that I felt pretty silly at first because I didn't feel like it. I didn't feel like praising. I just wanted to watch television or do something to get my mind off of what was going on around me and how mad I was at my husband at the time. But you know, I started singing and started laughing, and singing, and laughing, and realized that no matter what was thrown my way, the world or Satan could not take my joy away from me. I also realized Satan wanted to defeat me, but God allowed it for my good. My husband and I needed to know from the start that there would be testing. In the next few years, there would be more testing, and if we ran away every time things didn't go our way, we would always be running and not doing anything for God's Kingdom, always trying to make ourselves comfortable. That is not what we are called to do. But we were to stay the course. We were doing what God had called us to do. It was also one of the first times that God made me realize that a vital part of getting out of depression is to praise the Lord, whether with singing, or a time of being thankful for what you have, or what the Lord has done for you. You can't stay in the state of depression when your heart and mind is stayed upon Him. Go over things in the past where you know God was present in your life, where you could see His hand directly, and it will make things you are worrying about now come into perspective. Think of the family God has given you, or your home, things that, apart from God, you would not have.

I'll tell you something else; if you praise every time you go through times of trials—the times it is brought on by Satan—he will start to leave you alone. He does not want to cause you to start praising. Satan's plan is to keep people out of God's Kingdom and for those in God's Kingdom to lead defeated lives, so that we aren't influencing others for the Kingdom. If you use times of trouble as a trigger to remind you to praise, the next thing you know, Satan will be leaving you alone because He doesn't want to be the cause of anyone praising the Ruler of the Universe. Make it a practice to praise when things get tough. It won't come to you automatically at first, but before you know it, it will be one of the first things you do and then Satan will say, "Every time I throw something their way, they start praising the Lord. Let's just leave them alone. The last thing we want to do is cause any praise to go to God." Satan is looking to defeat

Christians because the more Christians He can keep knocked down, the less the Kingdom of God spreads.

When I thought I could not take it any longer, here are a couple of Scriptures that have also helped me. "No temptation has seized you except what is common to man. And God is faithful; He will not let you be tempted beyond what you can bear. But when you are tempted, He will also provide a way out so that you can stand up under it" (I Corinthians 10:13). Isn't God great to give us Scripture to let us know He will never leave us? Praise Him that you are not alone; others have faced it, too.

"Count it all joy my brethren, when you fall into temptations and trials, knowing that the proving of your faith works patience and let patience have its perfect work, that you may be perfect and entire, lacking in nothing" (James 1:2–4). Again, isn't God good, giving us so many Scriptures dealing with hard times? He knows us. He created us, and He tells us that, without these trials, we would not have the proving of our faith that works patience, so that we may be perfect (whole) and lacking in nothing. How great is that! Yet, it is a process we have to go through. I stated earlier that the world's advertising says we shouldn't have times of trials, struggles, or feeling down. God says to count it all joy. There is a bigger picture happening here in your life, and it will result in a more perfect person. We will be better off for going through trials. You have probably never had anyone tell you that you will be better off in the long run for going through trials. That's because the world and its knowledge is contrary to what the Bible tells us—what God has to say about it. The world would say, "Have self-pity. You deserve it." But the Bible says to count it all joy. The Bible is very clear, over and over again that there are times of trials, and the Bible even shares stories of men and women who struggled tremendously. I think of Naomi in the book of Ruth, who lost her husband and two sons. When she went back home, she told them to call her Myra because she was so distraught and depressed. She thought the Lord had left her.

And David, after his sin with Bathsheba, He realized the result was his son dying. God put these stories in the Bible so that we could see there were others, even men after God's own heart, who struggled. Yes, there are other valuable lessons in these stories, but we often overlook the fact that they were people, like you and me, who had struggles and despair, and, yet, they came out better than they were before, with the help of God watching out for them and protecting them. I know that in my most extreme depths of my depression, when I wanted to hurt my child, that I cried out to God, and I could feel His hand of mercy reaching out to tell me He was there for me. He would protect me from doing harm to myself or others, but I had to cry out to God in total desperation. Realize you don't have to let it get to the point of total desperation before you seek God. Start giving Him praise at the start, and watch as His Hand of mercy guides you in the path you need to go, or even leads someone to you at the point of your need. Trust God, and not in your ability, to take care of things. Praise Him. You will be amazed at the difference it will make in your heart, soul, mind, and strength.

◌⳾ Passages to Ponder

Psalm 34:1–4

II Chronicles 20:22

Psalm 150:2

Psalm 103:2–4

◌⳾ Practical Application

1. In the above passages what did you learn about how often you are to praise the Lord?

2. How does being in a spirit of praise affect your attitude?

3. In II Chronicles 20:22 what happened when the people began to sing and praise the Lord? How can this apply to you?

4. What does Psalm 103:2–4 say we are not to forget?

5. What does God forgive? Does He forgive some or all?

�🔑 Prayer

Write out a prayer asking God to give you a heart of praise, to not forget all that He is and all that He has done for you, and to not take it for granted.

⚷ Personal Reflections

CHAPTER 6

Proclaim

But I have prayed for you, that your faith may not fail; and you, when once you have turned again, strengthen your brothers.

Luke 22:32

What do you mean, tell others? Go around and tell everyone I am having panic attacks, or I am depressed? That I think I will never be happy again? That I can't pull out of this state of sadness? Or that I have the overwhelming feeling that I will never be happy? That I don't want to live my life this way, so why live at all?

The pride in us does not want to tell others. I don't know why that is; maybe we want to put on a front and pretend we are something we are not, that we have it all together, but inside we are dying and crying. Or maybe we think others will feel differently toward us or badly for us. In my case, I thought, if people knew, they might take my children away from me, or I would be separated from my family. I was having thoughts of killing my child, and by my telling I feared they might take her away. Yet, having violent thoughts about her shows that I was not thinking clearly on one hand, loving her so much on the other hand, not wanting her to be torn from her mother. But when I was able to share with someone, they pointed out how opposite my thinking was, that I was not crazy, but the thoughts I was having were. That helped me at that point more than anything, to know that others could see things from a different perspective and help me to see straight.

They still liked me. They were still willing to be around me. They still were willing to invest time in me and with me. I was not going to be left alone. Another way we sometimes deal with the depression is to build up walls due to fear of being left alone. We pretend we don't care what others think, so we build up walls to protect ourselves. Or we go against the flow of things, just to be different and put on a front: "I don't care what people think of me." But the truth is we do care. The harder we try to build up the walls and the more we try to act like we don't care, the more it becomes obvious that we are hurting and trying to protect ourselves from more hurt. People can see right through you; the only one you are fooling is yourself. You get so caught up in what is going on with you that you can't get out of the fog of your mind. It really takes someone who is willing to listen and put things into perspective for you because that is the last thing you are able to do, and that is OK. This is why God tells us to go to one another, pray for one another. I don't know what your reason for not telling others might be—there are many different reasons it could be. But it is very important to tell others.

There are reasons why you should not be afraid to tell others. By telling, you are also loosening the chains that Satan is trying to bind you with. Let me first start with this. By telling others what you are going through, you are not allowing Satan to have a stronghold in your mind. He will tell you lies, such as, "People will think you are crazy. They won't have anything to do with you." He knows the truth, which is the more Christians know, the more you will be covered in prayer. God Almighty will break the chains. I will tell you there are Christians who will say, "Just trust in the Lord, and you will be OK," but, yet, they are not willing to invest the time with you, be there for you, or listen to you. There are always people who are going to let you down, but when you run across them, just remind yourself that God knows what you are going through, and He has the right person who can minister to you best. If a Christian is not supportive, then just look at it as though he or she is not the person God has placed in your life for such a time as this. Tell others and keep telling others until you find the person who God has placed there for you.

God wants you to understand that, ultimately, He wants you to be solely dependent on Him. There will be times when He is all you have, and, now looking back, those times are the sweetest with the Lord because they drew me closer to Him. I know I have a deeper relationship with Him than I have ever had before, and, I also know, that if it weren't for those times I wouldn't have the assurance that I now have in my salvation and in my Savior. Satan will tell you things like, "They might take your children away or your husband will leave you. Your friends won't want to hang out with you if you are down all the time." Satan is a liar, and he will kill, steal, and destroy you, if you let him have control. Satan will throw all kinds of things at you, anything to keep you quiet because he wants to build on the lies and secrets. But if you tell others what you're going through, then there will be those who pray for you, and there will also be those who have gone through it before, like myself, who can share with you what they learned through the process and what they did to get through. It may very well be that God will use them to show you some things He would like for you to see in your own life. And, most importantly, God is still in the healing business. You can get through it, and you don't have to live a life of defeat. You can win this battle through Christ. It does not have to be a life-long sentence. It will also be encouraging that you will get through it, and you will be OK. It helps knowing that there are others who have gone through it, and you don't feel like you are the only one. By telling others, they will also be able to help you see things from a different perspective than what you are able to see right now and share Scripture with you to lift you up. So, please don't be afraid to share with others. There is nothing wrong with having these feelings.

I love James 5:16 that tells us, "Confess your sins to each other and pray for each other so that you may be healed. The prayer of a righteous man is powerful and effective." So, why not tell others so they can pray for you? The Bible tells us it is effective. In Rick Warren's book, The Purpose Driven Life, he makes this statement, "We only grow by taking risks, and the most difficult risk of all is to be honest with ourselves and with others." I like that statement because sometimes the reason we don't want to tell others is not Satan at all; it is our own selfish pride. We don't want others to know we are not perfect. But I've got news for you; they already know it. No one is perfect. I have found that people respect you a lot more if you are honest with them and let them know you have hurts and struggles. You are more approachable that way. People who appear to be perfect have very few friends.

Let's get back to the pride issue. The Bible tells us that pride comes before a fall. We have to ask ourselves, "Is part of my struggle due to pride?" The Bible also tells us that God hates pride.

Tell others in order to get your focus back on track. The world and all its advertising tell us to think about ourselves. If you have this, you will be perfect. If you look like this, you will be perfect. If you own this, you will be perfect. When you don't have all the things the world tells you will make you feel good, then you feel badly about yourself. If you do have all, you still feel badly about yourself because our true joy is not found in things of this earth, but in the Lord. By telling others, they will help you stay grounded and focused.

What is it you should stay focused on? Hebrews 12:2 tells us to keep our focus/eyes on Jesus, the author and perfecter of our faith.

There is one more reason to proclaim that I want you to realize. When you come out on the other side of depression, anxiety, and panic attacks, and they no longer have a hold on you, you have to tell others what Christ has done for you, how He has set you free, and the lessons you have learned. You may save someone from having to go through it as long as you or I did. That is why I am sharing with you now, so you might start putting into practice the things I have shared with you.

One promise I always lean on is found in II Corinthians 12:9, "My grace is sufficient for you, for my power is made perfect in weakness. Therefore, I will boast all the more gladly about my weakness so that Christ's power may rest on me." Again, God is so good to give us so much Scripture to lean on.

If you want something to proclaim and to lean on, read Psalm 91. It is only 16 verses, but it will encourage you and give you courage to go out and tell others how God is protecting you, guiding you, keeping you from losing it. Tell others how He is doing it now and how He has done it in the past.

I have said many times throughout the book to be accountable, or tell others, but, in order to do this, you have to have fellowship with others. The tendency we have, when going through depression, is to isolate and stay away from church or social settings, so others can't see what we're going through. So we don't have to smile when, really, we are dying inside, or have to explain why we haven't been seen around or dropped out of everything, to do as little as possible and see as few people as possible. I am telling you that it is the wrong thing to do. I know how hard it is to get up enough courage and strength to get yourself up and ready to be with friends, family, and fellow Christians. They can lift up, exhort, encourage, and pray for you, and even take your mind off of your struggles. In Romans, the Bible tells us not to "forsake the assembling of yourself with one another," and this is the reason.

Psalm 91

He who dwells in the shelter of the Most High will abide in the shadow of the Almighty.

I will say to the Lord, "My refuge and my fortress, My God, in whom I trust!

For it is He who delivers you from the snare of the trapper, and from the deadly pestilence.

He will cover you with His pinions, and under His wings you may seek refuge; His faithfulness is a shield and bulwark.

You will not be afraid of the terror by night, or of the arrow that flies by day;

Of the pestilence that stalks in darkness, or of the destruction that lays waste at noon.

A thousand may fall at your side, and ten thousand at your right hand; but it shall not approach you.

You will only look on with your eyes, and see the recompense of the wicked.

For you have made the Lord, my refuge, Even the Most High, your dwelling place.

No evil will befall you, nor will any plague come near your tent.

For He will give His angels charge concerning you, to guard you in all your ways.

They will bear you up in their hands, lest you strike your foot against a stone.

You will tread upon the lion and cobra, the young lion and the serpent you will trample down.

Because He has loved me, therefore I will deliver him; I will set him securely on high, because he has known My name.

He will call upon Me and I will answer him; I will be with him in trouble; I will rescue him, and honor him.

With a long life I will satisfy him and let him behold My Salvation.

Wow! What an awesome and great Savior we have. He cares for you and every detail of your life.

I have prayed for you, if you are reading this book, that you would find comfort and peace, but above all, you will come out of this in love with Jesus, the One Who is the Lover of your Soul.

⚷ Passages to Ponder

James 5:16
1 Peter 2:9

⚷ Practical Application

1. According to the James passage, what are we to do *with* one another?

2. What are we to do *for* one another?

3. What are the benefits of confessing and praying to and for one another?

4. What are we to proclaim according to 1 Peter 2:9?

5. This week make it a point to proclaim something that God has done for you to a different person each day.

⚷ Prayer

Write out a prayer asking God to give you an opportunity to tell others about Him, help you to realize when the opportunity arises, and give you boldness to carry this out.

⚲ Personal Reflections

CHAPTER 7

Physical

Or do you not know that your body is a temple of the Holy Spirit who is in you, whom you have from God, and that you are not your own.

I Corinthians 6:19

I am by no means a professional of any kind. What I am is a person who has been through depression, anxiety, and panic attacks. I dealt with it off and on for most of seven or eight years (half of the time I was so out of it, I didn't know or care if another day went by or not). But have been free of it for about 27 years, as of the writing of this book. I won't say much about the physical part, except for a few things that I feel are important, and that played a small role in my recovery. I say a small role, because God gets all the glory. God is the One Who made the physical body, the One Who pointed out these few things to me that made a difference in my recovery.

The first thing I want to say is that if you are on medication, don't take yourself off of it without being under a doctor's supervision. I have known women to start putting into practice the things I share in this book, such as a consistent time in God's Word, prayer time, praising, proclaiming, and they start feeling better than they ever have. I have had a few call me and say they have taken themselves off their medicine. Don't do it. When you have been on medicine, it changes the chemicals in your body. When you take yourself off of them, without doctor's supervision, you are asking for trouble. It never fails, they call a few weeks later with major trouble again. Also why would you change something that is working? Am I saying that you can't be healed without medicine? No, not at all. I know that Christ can do all things. As a matter of fact, I have had doctors tell me that I would have been diagnosed as manic depressive, but, to this day, I have not had to take any medicine—because of God's grace and mercy. What I am saying is if you are on medicine, and you are told to stay on it, follow doctor's orders.

People hate the thought of being on a pill every day for the rest of their lives, I understand, but don't look at it that way. Look at it as a daily dose of Jesus, reminding you that you are not in control of your life—He is. And it is a pill He has allowed us to have to help us feel better and to know that He is in control. I tell people to call it a "daily dose of Jesus—their Jesus pill."

Another thing you need to do is exercise. I know you have been told this time and time again, and either you don't have time, or you hate it, or you mean to, but you forget. Let me help you make it simple. If you can just do 10 minutes a day, it will help. Ten minutes where you get your heart rate up, jog in place in front of the TV to take your mind off of exercise, if you want. Keep it simple, but do something. There is a chemical in your body called serotonin. It is what the medical field calls the "mood-lifter chemical." When you get your heart rate up, your body releases this chemical into your brain, and it is a God-given mood lifter. God built us with natural mood lifters, again just telling me He knew we were going to have times like this. He built in a way for us to help ourselves not to stay in this state. Not to mention, you'll feel good about doing something good for yourself. If you are consistent with 10 minutes a day for about a month, you will, all of a sudden, find yourself fitting in an extra minute or two, and, before you know it, you will have worked up to 30 minutes a day. You will feel good, and you will also notice a few unwanted pounds have come off, helping you to feel even better about yourself. Find someone to hold you accountable, if you need to—anything to keep yourself consistent in all the areas we have covered in this book.

Eat right. I know you know this, but sometimes we need to be reminded, so I am reminding you. If you don't have the energy to come up with a balanced diet (I know when you're depressed, you are not always thinking straight or eating right), keep it simple. Have fruits and vegetables, ready to grab in your refrigerator, so when you look in to get food, they are already there and ready to eat. Buy the already chopped, ready-to-eat kind if you need to— anything to get you eating properly. When I was going through depression, I couldn't even do my dishes, so to prepare myself something nutritious would be unheard of; I could barely get out of bed. I remember many times thinking, "I have to eat, even if it is just a few bites to keep myself alive." The sad thing is, I would grab a sweet or junk food, which only fueled the depression. I was only getting one type of food— sugar, and not vitamins or protein. So, if I would have kept fruits and vegetables cut up and ready, I could have grabbed them, helping my mind to think more clearly. If you are malnourished, your mind will play tricks on you. It is very important to eat well.

Get the proper rest! What happens when you are depressed? You tend to sleep a lot because you know when you are sleeping, the fears, anxiety, and thoughts of worthlessness are gone. You don't have to deal with things while you are asleep. It is an escape. I can remember telling myself just to do what you have to do: "Sleep the rest of the day, and you won't have to deal with any thoughts and feelings." But I wish I had been told to keep myself up during the day, so I would be tired at night. What happens is you sleep any time you can, and at night you are wide awake. That is when your mind works overtime—when it is dark, and you have to be quiet, so you won't wake anyone else up in the house. You lay there and let thoughts and worries creep in. Stay awake in the day, so you will sleep at night. In order to fall asleep, have a good book, or better yet, read a couple of encouraging Scriptures before falling asleep, so your mind is on something other than yourself. If your mind starts to wander, start to pray. Remember some of the things I said earlier. Pray for God to show you what it is you need to address in your life that He can help you with and ask God to bring to mind someone who is hurting, so you can pray for them. Get your mind off yourself.

Limit social media. I have realized the more time I spend on social media, the more anxious I become. Why does it affect me so? It could be that I see people doing more than I can accomplish or having things that I don't have. Or people who are negative tend to make me see things in a negative way. It could be a number of things. I may be wasting time that I could be doing things that need to happen in my life.

What happens then is I forget that God created me to be me. Not someone else. God has blessed me with the things I have, not the things others have, and I am to be grateful. I also have things to accomplish for His Kingdom, and if I am constantly on social media, I waste a lot of time.

Above all, remember what God said in II Corinthians 12:8–10, "But He said unto me, My grace is sufficient for you, for my power is made perfect in weakness. Therefore I will boast all the more gladly about my weakness, so that Christ's power may rest on me. That is why, for Christ's sake, I delight in weakness, in insults, in hardships, in persecutions, in difficulties. For when I am weak, then I am strong."

To God be the Glory!

ℚ Passages to Ponder

Isaiah 43:7

Psalm 139:14–15

Genesis 1:27

Jeremiah 29:11

ℚ Practical Application

1. Whose image are you created in and what are you doing to create your own image instead of being a representative of God's image?

2. In the Isaiah passage whose name are we called by and created for? Who formed you?

3. Read Psalm 139:14–15. Were you an accident? Did God take time making you? How do you know?

4. According to Jeremiah 29:11, what does God know about your future and what are His plans for you?

5. How does knowing God's plan for your future help you to lean on Him and His purpose?

⚷ Prayer

Write out a prayer asking God to help you see how He has a purpose for your life and to give you the strength to protect your body and time so that it will reflect His image.

⚷ Personal Reflections

99379717R00070

Made in the USA
Lexington, KY
15 September 2018